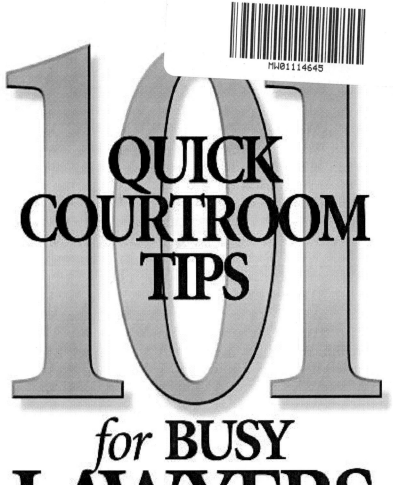

# 101
## QUICK COURTROOM TIPS
### *for* BUSY LAWYERS

## Bob Gerchen

**Legal Action**

Quick Courtroom Tips for Busy Lawyers

By Bob Gerchen

For more information contact:

Legal Action
6165 Delmar Boulevard, Suite 201
Saint Louis MO 63112
(314) 863-0909
http://www.CourtroomPresentationTips.com

ISBN 0-9768454-0-7
Library of Congress Catalog Card Number: 2005904394

10 9 8 7 6 5 4 3 2 1

Printed in the United States of America

The purpose of this book is to educate and entertain.  The author and Legal Action publishers shall have neither liability nor responsibility to any person or entity with respect to any loss or damage caused, or alleged to be caused, directly or indirectly, by the information contained in this book.

*If you do not wish to be bound by the above statement you may return this book to the publisher for a complete refund.*

*To those from whom I've learned
the most:  You know who you are,
but here are your initials, anyway.*

*EGO*
*RG*
*DB*


*and  CKR*

# Table of Contents

# The Golden Rule

*Never, ever underestimate the intelligence of jurors.*
*Most of the people you talk to you in a courtroom*
*are smarter than you think, and it's a guarantee that every one of them has at least one life experience that you don't have.*

# CHAPTER ONE

# *Courtroom Demeanor*

# BE YOURSELF.

Be yourself, not who you think a lawyer should look like, act like or sound like. In acting, we call this "getting out of your own way." The most important characteristic you can exhibit in the courtroom is accessibility. The only way to be accessible is to be yourself.

# SHARE OF YOURSELF.

There are natural barriers between those inside the "well" and those in the jury box. You're comfortable in the courtroom (we hope); to them, it's a foreign land. You speak "the language;" they do not. You're dressed up; they are not.

It's important to break down those barriers in order to develop rapport. One of the best ways to do that is by sharing of yourself. Throw in small, anecdotal facts about yourself. Especially in voir dire. If you're a little nervous, say so. Don't dwell on it, but let them know this case is important to you.

The more jurors see your humanity, the easier they will find iit to relate to you. Share of yourself so they can see inside a little.

# SHARE OF YOURSELF — BUT SPARINGLY.

Sharing a personal experience or something about your life – particularly in voir dire – can help build rapport with the folks you're talking to. A little bit here, a little bit there. But, self-revelation can go too far.

How far is too far? It's hard to say, but try to gauge it this way: If you're using the pronoun "I" more than twice a day after voir dire is over, you're probably turning the focus too much upon yourself and not enough on your client and the case.

# SOMEONE SEES EVERYTHING.

There are 12 people on the jury, plus at least a couple of alternates. So chances are, at least one of them sees every-thing that happens in the courtroom. If your client snickers when an opposing witness testifies, not all the jurors will notice, but one of them – or several of them – will. You need to be cognizant of that – and so does your client. That cognizance must begin in the parking lot. Someone sees everything. It's typical for attorneys and clients to drop their guards as a long trial drags on. But, everything is something, and someone sees everything. Make it a watchword among the trial team: Someone sees everything.

# FOCUS ON STAYING "OPEN" TO THE JURORS.

In the theatre, actors are admonished to "stay open." That means keeping your body positioned such that the audience can see your front, unless a dramatic element of the show dictates otherwise.

In the courtroom, remember that the jurors are the center of the audience and always "play" to them. When questioning a witness, turn your body so that you can face, and include, the jurors. Do the same at sidebars; instead of turning your back on the courtroom and talking directly to the judge, turn to the side so that the jurors can see your face and speak to the judge slightly over your shoulder.

It's all about including the jurors in your case as much as possible.

# When Choosing Between a Suit That Is More "Lawyerly" and One That Is More Comfortable, Go with Comfort.

"What!? Is he CRAZY?!" you might ask.

The answer is yes. But that's not the point. This tip goes back to being who you are, not who you believe a lawyer should be, or look like or sound like. I'm not saying that you should walk in looking rumpled and unshaven. Rather, if you wear something that isn't very comfortable (but is very lawyerly), your discomfort will translate to your courtroom performance.

# 8

# YOU DON'T HAVE TO BUTTON YOUR JACKET WHEN YOU STAND UP TO INTRODUCE YOURSELF TO THE JURORS.

# SOMETIMES YOU JUST HAVE TO LIGHTEN UP.

I was recently involved in a jury selection in a high-profile, high-intensity case. There were three parties, and the oral voir dire was being done in rounds. After Round One, we pinpointed a series of questions that needed to be asked, and I pointed out that, on the heels of an unexpected late hardship strike, one juror was coming up that was a potential cause strike, and he now needed to be talked to.

When it came time for my client's Round Two, he stood up and started asking jurors who they most admired in their lives and why. Then he asked about their favorite TV show. At first, I was tense – "What about Juror Number 91?!" I screamed inside. It became clear, however, that my client had read the room far better than I had; the jurors were tired. Including showing up to fill out questionnaires and ask for hardship, individual voir dire for cause and now general oral voir dire, it was Day Three of jury selection. They were tired of being probed and prodded. And the attorney got a lot more mileage – and gained a lot more rapport – by just "chatting them up" at that point. They loved talking about whom they admired, what values drove them to admire people and why they loved "Desperate Housewives."

Sometimes, you just have to lighten up.

# CHAPTER TWO

# *Language*

# THINK AND SPEAK LIKE THE PEOPLE YOU'RE SPEAKING TO.

Early in his career, a soon-to-be-famous lawyer tried what he believed was a masterful case. He had laid out his case clearly; he had directed his witnesses beautifully; his cross-examinations were on-point and scored many points; his closing was passionate and well-organized.

As he and opposing counsel awaited the verdict, they were informed that the jurors needed some questions answered before they could continue with their deliberations. Once all the parties were assembled in the courtroom, the foreman rose. "Your honor," he began, "There were two words that were used throughout the trial that we don't understand and we were hoping you or the lawyers could define them for us. The two words are 'plaintiff' and 'defendant.'"

It's all too easy to use words in a courtroom that you use in everyday practice. Keep in mind, though, that to jurors, words like "injury," "produce" and "appearance" have different meaning in everyday life than they do in a courtroom.

For example, a friend and colleague, Anne Graffam-Walker, who is a linguist and former court reporter, once worked a deposition in which she took down the following exchange:

*Attorney: Is your appearance here today pursuant to a deposition notice I sent to your attorney?*

*Witness: Um, no. This is how I dress when I go to work.*

It's an easy rule: When speaking to laypeople, speak in lay language.

# USE WORDS THAT EVOKE IMAGES. ADJECTIVES ARE USELESS.

Quick – define excruciating. Can you do it?

It's the most common adjective used in conjunction with the word "pain." And yet, it means nothing. Excruciating to one person is mildly annoying to another. How about, "Mr. Jones' head hit the windshield, and he experienced a pain that he'll tell you was like having a metal wedge being driven into his forehead with a sledgehammer."

Could you feel that?

# IT'S YOUR JOB TO EXPLAIN THE UNFAMILIAR IN FAMILIAR TERMS.

Often, attorneys will use a technical term – a medical term or insurance term, for example – and not bother to explain to the jurors what the term means.

It's easy to get comfortable with the nomenclature of your case, and to, subsequently, forget that most of the folks in the jury box are hearing many of these same terms for the first time. Be sure to explain unfamiliar terms in familiar language. While it increases juror comprehension of your case, it also will help raise your level of credibility.

# USE ACTIVE TENSE.

Here's my favorite example of a lawyer strangling the English language through use of passive tense:

*"Sir, what was your understanding of what the nature of the instructions were that were given to her by you?"*

That's a seven-word sentence in the hands of someone who uses active tense:

*"Sir, what instructions did you give her?"*

# DOES YOUR LANGUAGE INTIMIDATE?

If you introduce a case as "complicated," as in "This is a complicated case," most jurors will receive one of two messages: either, "I'm not going to understand this, so I won't even try," or "S/he thinks I'm stupid." If it's a complicated case, find ways to simplify your presentation.

# TIP 15
## BEWARE OF LANGUAGE THAT DISEMPOWERS.

If you preface your comments at closing with something like, "I'm sure you're tired of hearing lawyers talking," or "I'm almost done" or "I'm only going to talk another 10 minutes and then I'm going to shut up," (I've heard all of these sentences verbatim in courtrooms); you'll weaken the message that follows.

# TAKE THE ABSTRACT AND MAKE IT CONCRETE.

The best way to illustrate this point is to give an example – in other words, I have to make it concrete.

An acceptable level of a contaminant may be 10 ppb, or 10 parts per billion. But what does that mean? If we make it concrete, we could say that 10 parts per billion is the same as 10 manhole covers within the entire area of say, Seattle.

To make the abstract concrete, you need to find real-world analogies. Most people think that a 20-mph collision is a minor impact. But, if it were illustrated by this analogy, it would seem more significant:

"Take off running. Get up to full speed. After about thirty yards of going full speed, run into a brick wall. Did that hurt? A lot? Maybe you have a concussion? A few broken bones? You were moving at a rate of speed of about 12 mph."

# TIP 17
# WHEN REFERRING TO THE PARTIES, USE ARTICLES.

In court, many lawyers call the person who has brought the suit "Plaintiff," or the person against whom the civil or criminal action has been brought "Defendant."

If you use these words this way, it probably won't ruin your case; it's doubtful it's a deal-breaker. But, it is one more way of distancing yourself from the jurors by speaking a language that is different from theirs.

So – no big deal, but if you're going to call someone a name, use "the" in front of it.

# IT CAN BE DEATH TO TELL JURORS WHAT THEY "HAVE" TO DO, OR WHAT THEY "CAN'T" DO.

No one likes being dictated to.  It smacks of condescension, and it can easily backfire.

There are ways to soften a "have to" or a "can't."

**Bad**: "You might be tempted to split the difference. Well, you can't do that."

**Fair:** "You might be tempted to split the difference. Well, the law says you can't do that."

**Good:** "You might be tempted to split the difference. But the law tells us that we have to calculate damages independently, not by average."

In the bad example, you're dictating to them.

In the fair example, you've deferred to higher authority; it's not you telling them directly.

In the good example, we're joining with the jurors in deferring to higher authority; we're all in it together.

Recommend, ask.  Dictate at your own risk.

# THERE IS BEAUTY
# IN SIMPLICITY.

A law school education is the enemy of simplicity. It's amazing how attorneys will use four or five words when two will do, or throw around phrases such as "have the occasion to" or "Did there come a point in time ...?" or "What did you understand to be ...?"

My favorite story of a lawyer using simplicity beautifully goes like this:

Around the turn of the century (the 20$^{th}$ Century, that is), railroad companies, in hopes of stemming the tide of accidents at railroad crossings and their subsequent lawsuits, turned to a lawyer to write a warning that would spell out what the duties and responsibilities of pedestrians and those in wagons and motor cars would be at the crossings. They paid him $10,000 in advance (a monstrous fee at the time).

This is what he sent back:

**"Stop, Look and Listen."**

The railroad executives must have gone bananas – ten thousand dollars for FOUR WORDS!! And one of them was "AND!"

But guess what? Accidents at crossings went down. Payouts from lawsuits went down. And chances are, decades later, someone used those four words when teaching you the safe way to cross the street.

There is, indeed, beauty in simplicity. If two words will do, use two.

# MOST JURORS DON'T CARE ABOUT BURDEN OF PROOF.

Quick. Define "reasonable doubt" without using the word "doubt" in your definition.

It's more effective focus on your story than on burden of proof. Law professors might like it, but jurors would just rather know what happened.

# JURORS DON'T CARE ABOUT "PRUDENT."

First of all, outside of a courtroom, who in the heck even uses this word?

Prudent may be a legal measure; laypeople, however, are more likely to look at behaviors in terms of whether they were "logical," "appropriate" or "right/wrong."

Remember – think and speak like the people you're speaking to.

# TELL WITNESSES AND JURORS WHAT YOU WANT THEM TO DO, NOT WHAT YOU DON'T WANT THEM TO DO.

Jimmy Johnson has coached NCAA national champions and NFL Super Bowl champions. He has said that he always expressed his coaching advice in the positive. Instead of telling a player, "Don't fumble," he would say, "Protect the ball." And the player would think about protecting the ball, as opposed to thinking about fumbling. There's a big difference.

It's the same with witnesses. The human mind doesn't do a good job of hearing the word "Don't," as in "Whatever you do, don't think of a pink elephant right now."

So, while you're working at getting the image of a pink pachyderm out of your mind, remember to tell someone to "remember" instead of "don't forget" or to "look up" instead of "don't look down."

T
I
P
**23**

# LEARN FROM ROSS PEROT: NEVER SAY, "YOU PEOPLE."

Remember during the presidential campaign of 1992 when Ross Perot was speaking to the NAACP, and he referred to his audience as "you people?" Ouch. Bad choice of words, Ross.

Yet, sometimes, lawyers make the same slip. They look right at the individuals seated in the jury box and call them "you people."

Jurors are not a separate species. "You people" only serves to separate yourself from the folks from whom you can least afford to separated.

Use "folks" or "ladies and gentlemen" or even, simply, "you." But leave off the "people."

# CHAPTER THREE

*Platform Skills*

# SILENCE IS GOOD.

There's nothing wrong with silence. Silence is dramatic.
Silence is better than talking when you aren't prepared for
what's about to come out of your mouth. When you take a
pause, most jurors will use the silence to replay in their heads
that which has just been said. Saying nothing for a few
moments after a witness has uttered something vitally
important adds drama to the moment; it also gives the jurors
a few moments to replay and to digest what has just been
said.

# ELIMINATE MEANINGLESS WORDS FROM YOUR VOCABULARY.

It's better to allow the room to fall silent than to use thinking sounds or what my old voiceover instructor, Susan Berkeley, calls, "meaningless words." Eliminate the "ums," "uhs" and "ahs" from your vocabulary.

How do you do that? Practice your voir dire, your opening and your closing. Record yourself and listen to the tape. Use a pause instead of inserting thinking sounds.

Remember Tip #24: Silence is Good.

# AVOID "LAWYER CADENCE."

I'm not aware of any course in law school that teaches attorneys to speak four to five words, pause, speak four to five more words, pause, etc. But I hear it all the time: "lawyer cadence." And man, is it hard to listen to.

Lawyer cadence probably has its roots in the conduct of depositions, when lawyers find themselves picking their way through questions. But, it's an unnatural verbal pattern that can lull people to sleep. Since this book has no accompanying CD, I'll try to describe the pattern I'm speaking of. When I note pauses below, we're not talking about a quick pause to take a breath. We're talking big, honking, pregnant Harold Pinter-esque pauses. The kind of pauses into which we could insert the Third Movement of Bach's Violin Concerto in G Major.

*"How many of you here (pause) would say that just because (pause) an employee has a non-compete clause in his contract (pause, pause), he would be wrong in even talking to another company (pause, pause, pause) while he's under that contract?"*

Pauses are helpful in creating drama and in giving the jurors a moment to absorb what they have just heard. But, if these pauses show up in every, single sentence, it becomes a meaningless technique. Work on being conversational. Monitor your cadence in the courtroom. Spend a two-week trial speaking in "lawyer cadence," and you run the risk of losing your constituency to painful boredom.

# TIP 27     LISTEN TO YOURSELF.

Make sure you know what you sound like. You may be resistant to this idea, but if you actually do it, you'll be very glad you did. For a period of about one to two weeks, tape your end-of-telephone conversations. Then take the tape home and after dinner, settle in with your favorite drink and listen to yourself. Then, ask the following questions of yourself:

- Do I sound convincing?

- Do I sound confident?

- Do I speak smoothly, or do I speak in "lawyer cadence," pausing after each four words or so?

- Do I use an ABSOLUTE MINIMUM of thinking sounds ("um," "uh," "ah")?

- Do I sound sincere when I'm trying to sound sincere? (You'd be amazed at this one – so many of us think we sound sincere when we actually sound condescending.)

# PRACTICE DIAPHRAGMATIC BREATHING.

Have you ever watched a baby breathe? Their stomachs rise and fall with the breath. As babies, we naturally breathe deep, from the diaphragm. The diaphragm is the strong wall of muscle that separates the chest cavity from the abdominal cavity. It relaxes to allow breath to expand the chest and contracts to force air out.

How do you know if you're breathing correctly? First, get used to what diaphragmatic breathing looks like. When lying in bed, place a book on your stomach and breathe normally. The book should rise and fall. If it doesn't move much, focus on relaxing the stomach and just allowing air to drop down farther into your body. Visualize the breath dropping way down into your stomach and lower abdomen.

When you're standing, look in the mirror. Take a deep breath. Do your shoulders rise when you breathe in? If so, you're constricting the chest cavity and not getting as much oxygen into your lungs as you should. Focus on keeping your shoulders down, breathing in through your nose and out through your mouth. Keep your mouth closed as you breathe in, with your tongue slightly raised against the hard palate (just behind your teeth). Let your stomach expand as you draw breath in.

The better you breathe, the better you do everything – speak, think, move. It's a good bet  that the best athletes on earth are those who maximize the use of their breath. Jerry Rice knows how to breathe. So does Michael Jordan. Watch close-up tape of these extraordinary athletes and notice how they control their breath as they move. That's poetry in motion.

# Remember to "Center and Settle."

The moment before you start speaking at voir dire or opening is always the most tense. Scientific research has shown that just before public speaking, the heart rates of some people can shoot up as high as 220 beats per minute. So, you need to bring that energy under control before you begin.

Stand still with both feet squarely on the floor. Feel your weight over the balls of your feet. Look at the jurors for a moment. Make eye contact. Now, you've centered yourself and you've settled into the moment. You're ready to begin.

# THERE ARE WAYS TO HIDE YOUR NERVOUSNESS.

Nervousness is natural.  Actually, it's good for the blood to be pumping a little fast and for the adrenaline to be flowing; it keeps you on your game.

But what about when your nervousness is over the top?  What if you're shaking and breathing hard, and you've got to go on? Here are a few suggestions to keep you from looking like Tom Cruise in "A Few Good Men":

1. **Don't draw attention to your hands.**

2. **Leave notes on a table or lectern.**

3. **Adjust your center of gravity.**  If one of your legs is trembling, shift to the other; if they both are, move your feet back, lean forward a bit and use the lectern as a brace.

4. **NO caffeine.**

5. **Grasp the sides of the lectern.**  It's not exactly a power posture, but it keeps you in control and gives you some time to get settled.

# EYE CONTACT IS A CRITICAL COMPONENT OF CREDIBILITY.

If you had a high school speech teacher who told you that when you're giving a speech, you should look over the heads of your audience, please send me the address of that teacher so that I can go over and personally slap him/her.

If you want your audience to believe you (you do want them to believe you, don't you?), you've got to look each one of them straight in the eye. Often. Easier said than done, though, isn't it?

# EYE CONTACT TIP #1: INCLUDE EVERYONE.

There are only six to 14 people in the jury box – make sure you spend a little time with each of them as you deliver arguments. Many speakers speak only to the middle of an audience and the people on the ends are left out. Some speak over the heads of the first row to the people in the back. Make sure everyone gets your attention.

# EYE CONTACT TIP #2: JUST LONG ENOUGH.

How long should eye contact last?  About as long as it takes to shake someone's hand and look them in the eye.  Shorter than that and your eyes are darting around, and you miss making a connection.  Too much longer than that and you're staring and people get uncomfortable, even defensive.

# EYE CONTACT TIP #3: VARY YOUR EYE CONTACT.

Avoid going back and forth across the rows, like a typewriter carriage, or falling into a certain pattern of movement with your eyes. Vary your eye contact.

# Eye Contact Tip #4: Practice "Shooting Down the Hands."

An exercise that public speakers use in practice sessions can help make your eye contact more consistent.

You can't do this alone; you need a practice audience. An audience of four to six people, or even more, is optimal. As you speak, should someone start to feel "left out," that is, that you haven't made eye contact in a long time, that person will raise his/her hand. You respond by making eye contact and that person drops the hand. As you continue on, you "shoot down hands" as you go. And, you can start to get an idea of where the hands go up most often, so you realize where your eye contact weaknesses lie.

## TIP 36
## TO HELP MAINTAIN EYE CONTACT, WRITE YOUR NOTES **BIG.**

It helps you keep your place, too.

# HAVE A "BASE POSITION."

In other words, get used to standing still in front of the jurors, with your arms at your sides. We can call this the "base position." If you can stand still, your movement will have more meaning. After you gesture, walk somewhere, change positions in front of the jurors, etc., go back to the base position. Think economy of movement.

# MAKE YOUR MOVEMENT HAVE MEANING.

Standing behind a podium is visually boring. So (in state court, anyway), a lot of attorneys like to get out and move around a little. That's good.

But many of them tend to wander aimlessly, back and forth in front of the jurors. "Picketing the jury," I've heard it called. That's bad.

Movement needs to have three things:

- Motivation
- Destination
- Coordination.

**Motivation.** Have a reason for going somewhere. It simply may be to draw jurors' focus to your client or to the other party. It may be to reach an exhibit. It may be just to change the visual landscape. But, without a reason, you're just wandering.

**Destination.** Go somewhere and stop. If you want to move around during argument, pick three spots – near the podium, near one side of the jury box, near the other side of the jury box, and alternate where you go. But, once you get there, stop! Stand still for a while. Without somewhere to go, you're just wandering.

**Coordination.** Talking fast? Move fast. Making a strong point? Make a strong movement.

# GESTURE FROM YOUR SHOULDER, NOT FROM YOUR ELBOW.

If your elbow stays by your side when you gesture, it looks like you have flippers, not arms. Gesturing from the shoulder brings power to the gesture and commands the courtroom space.

# THE LECTERN IS A TOOL OF THE DEVIL.

There are two circumstances under which it is acceptable to stand behind a lectern (or podium):

1. You are in federal court;

2. You are terrified of the jurors.

If neither of the above is true, get out from behind the lectern. Turn it to the side, or on a 45-degree angle, if you need it for holding your notes. Let the jurors see you, come to trust you, see you have nothing to hide.

*(Thanks to David Ball)*

# RAISE THE EMOTION BY SPEAKING LOWER.

It's an old saw that if you want people to listen to you, speak softly. Unfortunately, some lawyers take that to mean that their entire opening or closing should be spoken at a volume level audible only to dogs. That's not quite the idea.

The idea is, if you've been speaking in a normal tone of voice, or even loudly, and you suddenly lower the volume, people tend to sit forward and listen more attentively. Used judiciously, it's a great tool for raising the stakes. For example:

*They can talk all they want about the mistakes my client, The Plaintiff, made; but let me tell you one thing about that (pause, much softer). She's owned up to those mistakes. And, she's paid for those mistakes. Now, it's time for them to own up, too.*

# USE REPETITION.
# AGAIN AND AGAIN.

Just because you said something, doesn't mean that everyone got it. Some of the jurors could have been distracted by someone walking into the courtroom, or by something that happened at home before they came to court. It's possible that they just weren't listening at that moment. If it's critically important, repeat it. Even if they heard it the first time, repetition puts emphasis on important points.

# CHOREOGRAPH THE BEGINNING AND ENDING OF YOUR OPENING AND CLOSING.

You probably don't like to read your opening and closing. You may not even like to open or close from notes. You may be more comfortable "winging it," at least to a degree. That's fine. But, your opening and closing can be more effective if you choreograph your beginning and ending.

I'm not suggesting you inject dance steps into it. But know where you'll be standing when you start. Plan where you'll be standing when you finish. What gestures will you use to anchor the jurors' responses? What about tone of voice or a pause before your final words?

It's a time-tested tenet of public speaking: start strong, end strong. Have the beginning and ending of your arguments to the jurors planned out will help you do just that.

# DRINK A LOT OF WATER DURING A TRIAL.

If you suffer from TB (tiny bladder), this tip could be problematic.  But, with the typical break coming every 1-1/2 hours, you should be able to get to the restroom in time.

The upside of drinking a lot of water is that it keeps you more alert by keeping you hydrated, helps counteract fatigue and maintains lubrication of your vocal cords so that when you rise to speak an objection after not speaking for a long time, you won't squeak.

# PROTECT YOUR VOICE DURING TRIAL.

If you lose your voice, or just compromise it, during a trial, where are you then?

Keep these no-no's in mind just before and during a trial:

- Avoid grunting while working out. It scratches the throat.

- If you smoke or drink, keep them to a minimum (sometimes an immense challenge). These habits are vocal irritants.

- Don't spend too much time in bars, where we typically have to talk louder to be heard (and, there's lots of smoke to irritate the vocal chords).

- Throat clearing slaps your vocal chords around more than is necessary.

- And, hey – lay off the karaoke until after the trial is over, okay?

# TIP 46

# FUEL THE MACHINE WISELY.

Being in a trial is like running a marathon – the amount of energy it takes slowly depletes you mentally and, ultimately, physically. That's why it's important to make sure the fuel you're putting in your body during the trial is optimal for helping you achieve your objective.

**Food:** Keep the protein intake high, the carbohydrate intake low. Feed your brain. Eat smaller meals four to six times per day. Snack on a protein bar during breaks.

**Alcohol:** Avoid it if possible, or least moderate. It throws off your sleep cycles and dehydrates you, depleting brainpower. It also dries out your vocal cords.

**Water:** It's the stuff we're made of. Drink at least 8-10 glasses of it a day.

**Caffeine:** It's the stuff trials are made of. Let your conscience be your guide.

# EXPECT TO BE "MURPHIED."

Stuff happens.  A witness is delayed.  Another witness says something unexpected.  An exhibit falls off the easel.  The technology gets balky.

Accept that such things can happen, and you won't come unglued when they do.  It'll be easier to take it in stride.

But, if the 36-inch monitor you've been using to show deposition video crashes to the floor, don't do what your high school speech teacher told you and try to ignore it.  Address it, make light of it and move on.  But say something, because you'd better believe the jurors are thinking about it.  So, until you've addressed whatever weirdness just took place and then redirected their attention to more relevant matters, they're not listening.

# CHAPTER FOUR

# *Trial Strategy*

T
I
P

# 48

# "WHAT THE PEOPLE BELIEVE, IS TRUE."

### ANISHINABE INDIAN PROVERB

So many times, as I've sat in the viewing room observing juror deliberations with client attorneys, I've heard this explosion: "Where in the heck did they get that?! How could that possibly be important?? That doesn't *matter*!"

Ah, but is it does. That's why we test cases. To find out what is important to the people who are most important. Ignore what they say is important at your own peril.

# REMEMBER THAT JURORS ARE "COGNITIVE MISERS."

Some lawyers believe that they should put every fact that is even remotely relevant into evidence, and "let 'em sort it out." Well, they do sort it out. But, in order to make sense of this jumble of unfamiliar information they've been asked to absorb in a short period of time (often without the benefit of notes), jurors rely on heuristics, or cognitive shortcutting.

In other words, jurors tend to cling to the facts that they can relate to through their own life experiences and understanding and disregard the rest.

So, rather than making sure "everything is in," it's better to think objective and story and to rely only on the facts that support your linear storyline. Sort it out for them.

*(Thanks to Merrie Jo Pitera)*

# GUARD AGAINST FALLING IN LOVE WITH YOUR CASE.

All too often I've seen attorneys summarily dismiss the facts and evidence that favor the other side, believing that their case is a "slam dunk."

Ask yourself, "If I were representing the other side, how would I try this case?" Ask that question of other lawyers. Run the facts by "civilian" friends and find out what they find to be significant for both sides. Do pre-trial research – a focus group, a mock trial. In short, get some perspective. Just because you think your case is bulletproof doesn't mean that it is. It's what the jurors think that's most crucial.

# Dramatic Interpretation #1: Think Story.

Every trial is more than a list of facts to be debated; it is a story. You have the responsibility to your client – and to the jurors – to reveal the narrative that makes up your side's case. You can do that through thoughtful analysis of the story of your case, through thematic development, through the use of effective storytelling techniques, particularly in opening and closing, and through the use of witness ordering that supports your story. The five tips that follow outline the elements of the story that you need to keep in mind every time you develop a case.

T
I
P
# 52

# DRAMATIC INTERPRETATION TIP #2: THINK OBJECTIVE.

It's important to think about objective at every juncture of a trial – what is your overall objective in the trial; what do you want to get out of each witness; what do you want the jurors to think, to feel? Having a clear objective before you start will help bring your trial preparation into focus and keep you from chasing down rabbit trails.

It might be worth writing the overall objective of the trial on a board in your office or war room. The objective is like a goal – it needs to be tangible and stated in positive terms. For example, let's say you have a criminal defense case and your client looks vulnerable. Your biggest hope is to keep him out of prison. Instead of stating that your overarching trial objective is:

*To avoid prison time for Jim.*

You'll want to state that objective in positive terms:

*To convince the jurors that prison time for Jim is too much punishment.*

*-or-*

*To persuade the jurors to recommend probation for Jim.*

# DRAMATIC
# INTERPRETATION
# TIP #3:
# THINK OBSTACLES.

What is in the way of achieving your objective?  What does the other side have?  What are their case strengths?  What are your case weaknesses?  These are all obstacles to consider when you're thinking your way through your case story.

---

# DRAMATIC INTERPRETATION TIP #4: THINK STAKES.

What is at stake here? What will you gain if you win? What will you give up if you lose? What will your client gain or lose? Again – trials are not just about the law; they are about exceptional events in the lives of human beings.

When you've elevated the stakes high enough, you give yourself (and the jurors) the commitment necessary to reach your overall objective. But be careful: Make sure that the stakes truly match what is at stake. If you ratchet up the emotional intensity in say, a contract case, you could touch off some serious eye rolling in the jury box.

T
I
P
**55**

# DRAMATIC INTERPRETATION TIP #5: THINK PLACE.

Give the jurors a sense of where the events of the case took place and what was going on around those events. Place encompasses not only physical location, but social conditions and expositional events.

Creating place can be as simple as a description, or a map of the site in question or showing pictures of the place where events took place.

Or, it can be more involved. Millard Farmer, who exclusively does death penalty defense cases in the South, makes it a point to visit the home of every one of his clients. He wants to sit where his client sat, eat where his client ate and listen to the voices of his family. For him, it creates a sense of empathy. For the jurors, it can create a new perspective, which is exactly what he needs to create when he's trying to humanize someone who is being demonized.

# DRAMATIC
# INTERPRETATION
# TIP #6:
# THINK RELATIONSHIPS.

A huge part of your job is to communicate to the jurors the relationships that exist between you and the people and the evidence in the courtroom. Think about what your posture (and by posture, I don't just mean standing up straight) indicates about your attitude toward your client, or toward the judge or toward the clerk. Be conscious of how you stand in front of a sympathetic witness; for example, does your posture indicate sympathy to the jurors?

# DRAMATIC INTERPRETATION TIP #7: THINK STARTING POINT.

Some stories are best told in chronological order. Some are best told from the point of crisis, followed by exposition, such as the movie *21 Grams*. The film, *House of Sand and Fog* began with denouement (the aftermath) and then proceeded to exposition and conflict. The movie *Memento* was told backward. It was a cool film, but it's probably not a great trial technique.

When creating your case story, ask yourself: If this were a movie, how would it open? What is Act I, Scene 1? Where is the best place to first bring the jurors – who know nothing about this case – into my story?

*(Thanks to Jim Lees)*

# HAVE A THEME — BUT MAKE SURE IT'S REALLY A THEME.

Much is made of the need for a theme, or themes, for a trial. So what is a theme?

The dictionary definition of theme is: "A topic of discourse of discussion, often expressible as a phrase, proposition or question."

A case fact is not a theme. A piece of evidence is not a theme.

Where do we find our themes? That's the fun part; we can develop themes from famous stories, songs, fairy tales, proverbs and even from quotes from witnessess or jurors.

Themes should be repeated often throughout the trial, especially in arguments. Your themes need to be introduced in voir dire, stated and expounded upon in opening statement and woven into witness testimony, both direct and cross.

Here are some examples:

| | |
|---|---|
| Not a theme: | *"They told him they would honor the contract."* |
| A theme: | *"The Measure of a Man Is How Well He Keeps His Word."* |
| Not a theme: | *"His contract says he can be fired for an act of dishonesty."* |
| Theme: | *"The Contract is the Ultimate Authority."* |
| Not a theme: | *"The hospital discharged her too soon."* |
| Theme: | *"What a Difference a Day Makes."* |

# TIP 59   HEADLINE YOUR CASE.

In opening statement, it's critical to get jurors' attention before really tell them anything. Especially if you're the plaintiff or the prosecution. The jurors are still strangers in a strange land. It's possible that they just came out of the jury selection process and, pow! The trial is starting. They're getting settled in. They're
wondering how long this is going to last. They're replaying the arguments with their spouses from earlier in the morning. You need to interrupt them and get them tuned in.

This doesn't get their attention: *"This is a case about ..."*

Or, how about? *"I want to give you a road map ..."*

Or, even better, *"On behalf of my client, I want to thank you ..."*

In advertising, a headline is the ad for the ad. It is designed to interrupt a reader's/ listener's/viewer's alpha state and snap them into active listenings, or beta mode. Here are a few famous examples:

*Own a Gold MasterCard? A Premier Visa? Not After You Read This, You Won't*

*Is the Life of a Child Worth $1 to You?*

*Last Saturday, We Were Robbed. Where the Hell Were the Police?*

The ad copy then says, "Okay, you're paying attention. Now, I have some worthwhile, interesting information to give you about this topic."

Your case needs to have a headline, too. Boil your case down to its essence and say a sentence that will make your jurors want to sit up and listen. Some of the better ones I've heard over the years:

*Jane Madsen sees two of everything.*

*We all remember where we were on 9/11. So does Alice _____. She was face down, underneath her car, wondering if this was how she was going to die.*

*Jack _____ wasn't fired for being gay. Jack wasn't fired for being late. Jack wasn't fired for talking about his lover's illness. Because you see, Jack wasn't fired.*

---

# GIVE THE JURORS SOMETHING TO HOLD EVERY DAY.

Everyone gets to handle stuff in the courtroom – the judge, the clerk, the lawyers, the witnesses. The jurors don't get to handle stuff.

Let them be a part of your side of the case; give them something to hold each day – a copy of a document, perhaps a piece of deposition transcript (if allowable). Something. Giving them something each day is like taking them into your confidence.

*(Thanks to Robert Muth)*

# TIP 61    USE REPETITION.

There are a lot of facts you'll be asking jurors to assimilate in a relatively short period of time. You may have had the case for one, two or more years. They get exposed to it for two days or two weeks. So, if something is important, repeat it. Repeat it during voir dire. Repeat it during opening. Repeat it during closing. Don't assume that just because you said it once, they got it. Repeat it.

# If It's a Choice Between a Long Opening or a Long Closing, Open Long, Close Short.

Some attorneys will say, "I'm not great in opening, but I'm strong in closing," or "We'll give it all to them in closing." Too late.

Opening statement is a critical time for you. It's the time to give jurors a cognitive framework through which to evaluate the case. If you're on the defense side, your opening becomes doubly critical.

Open long, close short. As my friend, Karl Blanchard, said of closings, "There are damn few conversions after 25 minutes."

# THE OBJECTIVE OF CLOSING ARGUMENT IS DIFFERENT FROM WHAT YOU WERE TAUGHT IN LAW SCHOOL.

The trial framework you got in law school was that you lay the facts out in your case-in-chief and in cross-examination of opposing witnesses; and then in closing, you can sew it all together and tell the jurors what it all means. After all, they've been told not to form an opinion about the case until after they've heard all the evidence, right?

Jurors are not machines; you can't realistically expect them to just "log in" evidence as they hear it and then wait until later to draw conclusions (unless you're trying a case in Minnesota). Most jurors are leaning one way or the other by the time you get up to close.

So what good is closing? Well, your closing has three major objectives:

1. Give all of the jurors a reason to pay attention and to listen, in hopes that they may hear something that will influence their decision-making.

2. Give the jurors who are on your side specific, thematic ammunition with which to argue on your behalf.

3. Sway the undecided minority.

---

# T I P 64   PREPARATION IS KING.

*"The will to win is worthless if you do not have the will to prepare."* – Unknown

I've worked with hundreds of lawyers. The most successful among them have their own special strengths. Some of them have huge courtroom presence. Some of them are just incredibly likeable. One of them can break a bad venire like no one who has walked the earth. But, no matter what their discrete strengths were, they all possessed one central trait: An obsession with preparation.

# CHAPTER FIVE

# *Jury Selection*

# THINK IN TERMS OF "JURORS," NOT "JURIES."

A jury is not a monolithic entity. It's a collection of individuals, each with his/her own attitudes and life experiences. It's your job to explore those attitudes and experiences during voir dire.

# Ask Yourself, "What Are the Weasels?"

"Weasels" are case facts that could jump up and bite you in the butt (some might call them "landmines"). Taking a hard look at your case – looking at it as if you were preparing the other side, bouncing it off of friends who are laypeople (or "civilians," as I call them), doing some sort of pre-trial research – will help you identify the elements of your case that are most problematic.

What to do once you've identified these elements? Work them into your voir dire and get people who respond to your "weasels" to speak up and talk themselves off of the jury.

# TIP 67

# VOIR DIRE HAS THREE PURPOSES:

1. Learn about your jurors' attitudes and experiences.

2. Find the bad jurors and send them home.

3. Advance your case themes.

Thus, your job is threefold:

1. Get them to talk.

2. Get them to talk freely about themselves.

3. Get the right ones to talk themselves off the jury.

Do your job, and you'll find yourself arguing more of your cases to sympathetic jurors.

# TIP 68

## IN VOIR DIRE, WE DON'T WANT TO KNOW IF JURORS THINK THEY CAN BE FAIR AND IMPARTIAL!!

The purpose of voir dire is to ferret out those individuals who would be pre-disposed to being hostile to your case. Thus, we want to know when they are unfair and partial. If that happens to be when a client like yours has come before them to be heard, it's time to send them home.

# "Shut Up and Listen."

If you talk more than you listen during voir dire, you're not doing voir dire right.  As my friend, David Ball, says, "Shut up and listen!"

# TIP 70

# BE THE MOST INTERESTED PERSON IN THE ROOM.

Most people like to talk about themselves. They are more likely to talk about themselves when someone is truly interested in what they say.

Do you want jurors to open up to you? Be interested. Lean in. Look them in the eye. Ask follow-up questions. Most of all – *pay attention*. If you're looking through your notes while a juror is answering a question that you just asked, you're communicating to her/him that what s/he has to say isn't very important. And, that you're not very interested.

# TIP 71  ASK JUROR-CENTERED QUESTIONS.

We've already established that voir dire is effective only when you get the jurors to talk freely (as possible) about themselves. Yet, many lawyers ask questions in voir dire for which the only answer is agreement with the lawyer. And, they don't learn anything useful.

The questions you ask the jurors need to focus on them – their attitudes, their beliefs, their experiences. Here's an example:

**Terrible:** *"Does everyone agree with me that a doctor should use reasonable care when dealing with a patient and making a diagnosis?"*

The only answer to that one is a head nod. Or, nothing.

**Bad:** *"Do you expect a doctor to be reasonable and caring?"*

You're still asking, "Don't you agree with me?" The only acceptable answer is "Yes."

**Okay:** *"How do you know your doctor is being reasonable and caring?"*

You've opened up the question a little, but all they can talk about is reasonable and caring.

**Good:** *"When you go to a doctor, or take your child to a doctor, what do you expect of that doctor?"*

This question truly focuses in on juror experiences and beliefs. The answer may be one that speaks your theme of reasonable and caring. Or, you may find out the difference between jurors who take their doctors' word as gospel versus those who question everything regarding their health care.

*(thanks to Lisa Dahl)*

# TIP 72

# HAVE A SECOND PAIR OF EYES WHEN DOING VOIR DIRE.

Your job during voir dire is to establish a dialogue with the jurors. If you're constantly stopping to make notes, you interrupt the flow. Get out in front of the podium and talk to these folks. Meanwhile, have an associate, a paralegal – or if you're a solo practitioner, a family member – someone, take notes and watch jurors.

# GET EXACT QUOTES FROM JURORS.

Whoever is taking notes for you during voir dire needs to write down direct quotes when a juror says something that is particularly hostile to your side. When arguing for a cause strike, it's one thing to say, "Your honor, Mr. Jones indicated that he had a problem with my client because of his financial background," and quite another to say, "Your honor, Mr. Jones admitted that he can't give my client a fair trial because, and I quote, 'People who file bankruptcy bring it on themselves. They're irresponsible.'"

# BE SURE TO WATCH THE WATCHERS AS WELL AS THE SPEAKERS.

During voir dire, you can pick up a lot about jurors' attitudes when they are *not* speaking. Keep an eye on the folks who are around the person who is answering your question, or the question of opposing counsel. You may see a smile, a nod, a grimace, a widening of the eyes that calls for a follow-up with that particular juror. ("Mr. Smith, I noticed you had a strong reaction when Ms. Thompson said ____. Could you tell me a little about what you were thinking?"

# If You Have to Move to Strike a Juror for Cause While They're Still in the Box, Be Gentle.

Take the approach that you're helping him/her find a case that is better suited to his/her personality and experiences. Rather than accusing the juror: "Your honor, obviously Ms. Brown can't be fair in this trial. We ask that she be excused," try a kinder, gentler tack: "Your honor, Ms. Brown's comments indicate that she would be uncomfortable sitting on a jury in this case. We ask that she be excused so that she can have the opportunity to sit for a case with which she is more comfortable."

# TIP 76

## ENLIST AS AN ALLY THE JUROR YOU'RE ABOUT TO TRY TO BOUNCE FOR CAUSE.

Use leading questions that direct the juror toward one and only one conclusion: He/she is in the wrong courtroom.

*"You're uncomfortable about that, aren't you?"*

*"And, even if the judge instructed you that you're not supposed to consider my client's previous financial difficulties, you'd have trouble getting around that, wouldn't you?"*

*"So you wouldn't be able to be totally fair to both sides in this case, right?"*

*"Would it better for you, then, if you had an opportunity to sit on a jury for a case that you're more comfortable with?"*

Then: "Your honor ..."

# MAKE YOUR STRIKES TO THE JURY, NOT TO THE JUDGE.

This is a tough one. If you have to make your strikes in open court, it is a lot easier to stand up, look at the judge and say, "Your honor, we'd like to thank and excuse Juror Number Eight." And, that uncomfortable part of your life is over.

Here's a radical idea, though: instead of talking to the judge, look right at the juror. Smile, nod, perhaps even add a personal comment ("Now you get to leave early for that vacation."). It will make the excused juror feel less rejected (even when someone wants off the panel, there's a feeling of rejection when excused), but more importantly, the jurors who remain will remember how you handled it.

# TIP 78

# REHEARSE YOUR VOIR DIRE.

Why wouldn't you? It's your first, direct contact with the jurors – shouldn't you be extremely confident of what you're about to say? Find laypeople on whom to practice, and take an hour to rehearse. You'll find it to be an invaluable hour spent.

---

# CHAPTER SIX

## *Witnesses*

# TIP 79

# REMEMBER THAT TESTIFYING IS AN UNNATURAL ACT.

What if you were at a cocktail party and you were having a conversation with two other people, and each time Person #1 asked you a question, you had to direct your answer to Person #2, who could only stand there and look at you without saying anything?  And then, what if Person #3 were standing off to the side and when Person #1 asked you another question, said, "I don't think you should answer that." And then, Person #4, who was standing off to the other side, said, "Go ahead, you can answer that," and so you answered to Person #2, who just stood there mute and stared at you.

For those who are unaccustomed to testifying, it's a weird experience.  Going into your prep sessions with this simple truth in mind will make you more empathetic and better prepared to guide the witness to a level of comfort in testifying.

# BEGIN WITNESS PREPARATION BEFORE DEPOSITION.

So many attorneys are willing to spend all sorts of time prepping witnesses for trial, but they don't take much time to prepare them for depositions. If you wait until after the depo to prepare the witness, you often can be too late.

Sure, it's time-consuming. Sure, it's inconvenient. And, it's not realistic to be able to prep every single witness at length before depositions. But why wait until *after* your key witnesses have committed to testimony in deposition to prepare them?

Depositions are the verbal equivalent of Chinese water torture. The same questions. Over and over. No referee. And, it's unfair. It's like a beginning Golden Gloves boxer going 12 rounds with Mike Tyson. He's going to take a beating.

Help out your witnesses ahead of deposition, and help out your case.

# TIP 81

## THIS IS NOT WITNESS PREPARATION.

*(Begin at 12:55 for a 1 p.m. depostion)*

Listen carefully to the question.

If I object, stop talking.

Answer just the question you're asked.

Don't talk too much.

Don't volunteer anything.

Don't be nervous (Don't think about a pink elephant).

Okay, ready?  Let's go.

*(apologies to Eric Oliver)*

# TIP 82

# WHEN PREPARING A WITNESS, PARTICULARLY A LAY WITNESS, TO TESTIFY, ATTEND TO THE WITNESS' AGENDA FIRST.

Have you ever found yourself saying, "I told him what to say; he just didn't listen?"

Exactly.

So why didn't he listen?

It's easy to tell a witness what they can or can't say on the stand. It's easy to explain what the vulnerabilities of the case are and what the themes and message points are. But, unless you've first addressed the witness' issues, your instructions are likely to fall on deaf ears.

Testifying is an unnatural act. Most laypeople approach the experience with nervousness, trepidation and outright fear. Fear of humiliation, fear of tanking the case, fear of being made to look like a liar. It's important that your witnesses understand that you understand what they are going through.

So, instead of starting with, "This is what you've got to do ...," try starting with, "How are you feeling about all of this?"

# WHEN GIVING A WITNESS FEEDBACK DURING PREPARATION, POINT OUT GOOD POINTS FIRST.

In order to get your witness to make the adjustments you want him/her to make, you first have to make him/her want to listen. Giving positive feedback first puts him/her at ease and makes him/her more willing to listen to what you have to say about what you want changed or improved upon.

# In Practice Q & A, Give the Witness One or Two Points to Focus on at a Time.

You've done some Q & A with a lay witness. You take a pause in the exercise. And you say, "Okay, that was pretty good (a little weak, but it is leading with positive feedback). Now, I want you to remember to keep your eyes up, talk a little slower, look me in the eye when you answer and feel free to move your hands a little. You look a little constrained. Oh, and don't call it a loan; it's an advance. They'll chew you up on cross-examination if you call it a loan."

And, your witness starts eyeing the door.

How about, "I liked the way you answered directly – that's good. Remember now to use the word 'advance' instead of 'loan,' and be sure to look me in the eye when you answer."

Enough. Try it again.

# USE YOUR WITNESS' LANGUAGE.

Who hasn't had the frustrating experience of trying to get on the same page as a witness?  Who hasn't had to struggle to get a witness to understand a question?  Or, to understand a witness' answer (especially and expert)?

If your witness doesn't understand your question, or your terminology, ask the witness how s/he would phrase it, or what word s/he would use.  It'll help you avoid crossed signals on the stand.

Besides, it doesn't look good if an attorney and his/her witness are silently fighting over terminology.

# TIP 86

# WHENEVER POSSIBLE, MAKE A COURTROOM VISIT WITH YOUR CLIENT AND/OR KEY WITNESS.

Whether your client is the plaintiff or the defendant, the courtroom can be a daunting place. And, if the first time your client sees the courtroom and sits in the witness chair is the day s/he testifies, it can even make him/her more nervous.

Ease some of the pressure by walking through the courtroom with your client. You don't have to take this time yourself – an associate or paralegal can carry out these duties – but the client should get the lay of the land in advance. Show him/her where they will be sitting during trial (if s/he will be at counsel table); have the witness make the walk from counsel table or from outside the courtroom to the witness chair and get settled; show the witness where the restrooms are.

This tip may not seem like a big deal, but keep in mind that contrary to how they are instructed, jurors are making judgments – about you and your client – from the outset of trial. If your client has spent a little time in the courtroom and has already sat in the chair, the jurors will see someone who is more relaxed and confident, instead of someone with the "deer in the headlights" look.

# TIP 87 — MAKE YOUR ORDER OF WITNESSES INTENTIONAL.

Particularly in longer trials, it seems that lawyers decide on witness order by this question: "Who's available tomorrow?"

What a blown opportunity! While you certainly have to allow for the fact that some testimony will run shorter or longer than expected and court days can be truncated for one reason or another, you still must have a witness-order plan and try to stick as close to it as the exigencies of trial allow.

You have a story to tell. Each witness plays a role in that story. And, as mentioned earlier in this book, it's critical to keep in mind where your story begins and ends. Then order your witnesses by how you want to tell the story.

# Make Sure Your Witness Does This First Thing when Getting on the Stand.

What's the first thing a witness should do when arriving to testify? Settle in? Get comfortable? Adjust the microphone? How about, acknowledge the jurors?

When your witnesses walk to the stand, it is critical that they make contact with the jurors – look at them, smile at them, even say "hello" – to make sure that the jurors know the witness acknowledges them as the most important people in the room.

That's because they are.

# Make It Easy for Your Witness to Look at the Jurors.

I once had a tremendous argument with an attorney in Minnesota who insisted that jurors prefer to be spectators to a conversation between the lawyer and the witness.

Not so.

Communication research has shown definitively that one of the major credibility cues for a witness is eye contact with jurors. In my own experience, as I've spoken with hundreds of jurors about their impressions of witnesses they've seen, never once has anyone said, "I wish he wouldn't have looked at us so much." But I have heard, "I didn't trust him; he wouldn't look at us."

So, how do you make it easy for your witness to make eye contact? It's all about placement. Get away from the podium (or take it with you). Stand at the far corner of the jury box (the "x" marks the spot). This way you can have a conversation with your witness and include the jurors. Conversely, if you are cross-examining, you'll want to stand somewhere where the witness' focus will be pulled away from the jury.

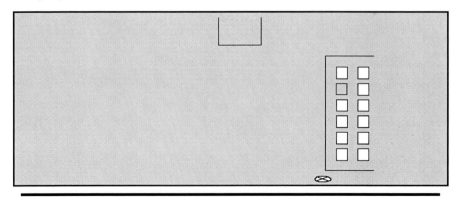

# USE REPETITION.

If a witness says something that bears repeating, repeat it for him/her. If it's a particularly weighty point, look at the jurors while you repeat it. If you want the witness to repeat it, and would rather avoid an "asked and answered" objection, wait a little while and say, "A bit earlier, you testified that (blah, blah), right?"

# HAVE YOUR OBJECTIVES IN MIND BEFORE YOU BEGIN CROSS-EXAMINATION.

What do you need this witness to admit? What do you have in mind for impeachment? What theme do you want to impart through this witness? Once you've achieved these objectives, sit down. Which leads us to our next tip ...

# BEATING THE CRUD OUT OF A WITNESS DOES NOT MEAN THAT YOU WON CROSS-EXAMINATION.

It depends on what your objective is – or should have been. F. Lee Bailey always said that he would never get mad at a witness until he could see that the jurors were mad at him. Beat the crud out of a sympathetic witness and it might bring you kudos from your colleagues for having "run rings around him logically," but it won't win any points with the folks who count – the jurors.

# TIP 93

# WHEN CROSS-EXAMINING, KNOW WHEN TO QUIT.

I've seen it too many times; an attorney has scored the points he needs to score on cross-examination; and now, smelling blood, asks just one (or two or three) questions too many. He loses momentum; the witness scores. And the cross goes, "Phhhhhhht."

The most famous example of taking a cross-examination too far follows:

Q: Doctor, before you performed the autopsy, did you check for a pulse?

A: No.

Q: Did you check for blood pressure?

A: No.

Q: So, then it is possible that the patient was alive when you began the autopsy?

A: No.

Q: How can you be so sure, Doctor?

A: Because his brain was sitting on my desk in a jar.

Ouch. Most lawyers would quit here and sit down, feeling a bit sheepish. Others, however, know no such shame. Let's watch as our hero continues digging.

Q: But, Doctor, could the patient have still been alive nevertheless?

A: It is possible that the patient could have been alive and practicing law somewhere.

One too many questions. "Phhhhhhht."

---

# MAKE SURE THE QUESTION IS RESPONSIVE TO THE ANSWER!

Yes, you read that right. Too often, an attorney will put a question to the witness and then consult notes or mentally log the next question while the witness is answering. What happens if your witness misses something that needs follow-up? What happens if an adverse witness says something unexpected?

In short, while an examination outline is important, so is the flexibility to deviate from the outline in order to respond to the witness' answers.

So: Listen, then ask.

*(Apologies to Eric Oliver)*

# CHAPTER SEVEN

# *Exhibits*

# EACH EXHIBIT SHOULD HAVE AN SCO — SINGULAR COMMUNICATION OBJECTIVE.

Some exhibits just get too, too fancy. Too much information in too small a space. Step back from any exhibit and ask, "What am I trying to communicate here? What is the one main point I want the jurors to take away from seeing this piece?" If you can't pinpoint a singular objective, you need to break down the exhibit into easier-to-digest components.

# TEST EACH EXHIBIT
# BEFORE YOU USE IT.

Know how far it is from your presentation media to where the farthest juror sits. If you don't know, find out – send someone to the courthouse to measure. If the trial is out of town, send local counsel, talk to the court clerk, something. This is critically important. What use is a brilliant exhibit if no one can see it?

Test readability at that maximum distance. If it's a moving exhibit (a PowerPoint, for example), test it before using it. Run through your argument with whomever is going to run the exhibit for you; or if it is an exhibit that will accompany witness testimony, run through it with that witness.

Rehearsal can preempt a multitude of sins.

# TECHNOLOGY CAN BE YOUR FRIEND.

There are a lot of great technological tools out there for trial lawyers, these days – Trial Director™, Sanction, Practice Master, etc. Take the time to learn one of the programs – or hire or retain someone who can do it for you. I've encountered a lot of attorneys who – aside from being technophobes – fear that jurors will hold it against them if they use a lot of technology; they're afraid they'll come off too fancy or too well-heeled.

Yet, when we ask jurors about their reactions to displays of technology in the courtroom or in a mock trial, invariably the response is that they are grateful for the clarity that the exhibits provide.

We live in an age of technology. Jurors are okay if courtroom presentation reflects that reality. If it clarifies your case, use it.

# BE CAREFUL NOT TO FALL IN LOVE WITH TECHNOLOGY.

It's amazing how many bells and whistles there are on our modern tools – "stuff" they do, just because "they can." It's cool – and it can be a trap.

Take, for example, the feature of most trial management software that allows a deposition to beplayed, along with the transcript scrolling beneath it. Be careful how you use it, though. Most people tend to watch the scrolling words, as opposed to watching the witness. So, the basic rule here is:

– If you want to educate (or if the words are hard to hear), show the transcript.
– If you want to show the lies, hide the transcript.

# LEAVE DOCUMENTS ON THE SCREEN LONG ENOUGH FOR JURORS TO READ THEM.

One of the biggest complaints we hear from jurors about documents in evidence is that the attorney puts up a document, reads about half a sentence from it and then whisks it away immediately. Jurors have told us that it makes them wonder what you're trying to hide when you do that.

Give the jurors enough time to read the document – even if it's only a couple of sentences. You can read it verbally faster than they can read it silently. Let it stay up for a few extra moments so that their eyes can catch up with your voice.

# DEVELOP A RELATIONSHIP WITH EVERY PIECE OF EVIDENCE.

This isn't as racy as it sounds.

We all remember the *Rodney King* trial. One of the key pieces of evidence was the baton of Officer Timothy Wind. Interestingly, everyone who picked up that baton communicated a different relationship with it. The prosecutors held it with two hands and swung it around a bit, making it look as menacing as possible, while the defense tended to handle it more casually, communicating that it was simply a tool of the trade.

The way you handle evidence communicates a great deal to the jurors. If a document is extremely important, it's incongruous if you handle it casually. Hold it as if it were a newborn baby. Show reverence for this piece of evidence and the jurors will, at the least, want to know more about it, know what it is about this document that warrants such special treatment.

---

# ONE LAST TIME

 **Use Repetition.**

Get the idea?

*(Big thanks to Pete Rowland)*

# If You Enjoyed ...
## *"101 Quick Courtroom Tips for Busy Lawyers"*
Pass This Form Along to a Colleague or Friend...
Or Consider Ordering Additional Copies As Gifts!

## Great Gifts for:
- **Friends**
- **Summer Interns**
- **Colleagues**
- **Incoming New Lawyers**

| | Quantity | Price | Total |
|---|---|---|---|
| Additional Copies of *101 Quick Courtroom Tips for Busy Lawyers* | | 34.95 | |
| *101 Quick Courtroom Tips for Busy Lawyers* CD Audiobook | | 26.95 | |
| Quantity Discount on orders of 3 or more (paperback or audio): 10% | | | |
| Subtotal | | | |
| Shipping and Handling Books: $4.95 first book, $1 each additional **Order 10 or more books = Free Shipping** Audiobooks: $1 each CD | | | |
| MO residents add 8% sales tax | | | |
| Total Order | | | |

Name _____

Address _____

City/State/Zip _____

Phone _____

Email _____

☐ Check  ☐ Purchase Order  ☐ Visa
☐ MC  ☐ Amex  ☐ Disc

Card # _____

Exp date _____

Name on card: _____

**Order Now!**
Tel: 314-863-0909
Fax: 314-863-8787
We Accept:

Order online via secure server
www.
CourtroomPresentationTips.com

Mail:
6165 Delmar Blvd., Suite 201
St. Louis MO 63112

# About the Author:

**Bob Gerchen** is a trial consultant and former actor based in St. Louis, Missouri. In his trial consulting practice, he specializes in helping attorneys sharpen their courtroom communication skills. His work with trial lawyers focuses on platform skills, juror rapport, storytelling techniques and witness preparation.

In addition to his active training practice with various legal associations, he spends a great deal of time working one-on-one with attorneys, honing their oratorical skills for openings, closings and argument before the bench.

Bob brings 20+ years of experience as an actor, director and public speaker to the trial consulting arena. He has appeared in feature films with Bette Midler and Burt Reynolds, and was a recurring Guest Star on the prime-time television show, Miami Vice.. Bob also has appeared in over 50 commercials and over 300 industrial and educational films, either onscreen or as an announcer.

Bob conducts legal education seminars based on the topics covered in this book. For a list of upcoming seminars, visit www.CourtroomPresentationTips.com. To arrange a specialized seminar for your firm or law association, you can contact Bob at:

**6165 Delmar Boulevard**
**Suite 201**
**St. Louis MO 63112**
**(314) 863-0909**
**rgerchen@litigationinsights.com**